Thanks for the tragedy

Katherine Cullen

BookLeaf Publishing

India | USA | UK

Presentation by *BookLeaf Publishing*

Web: www.bookleafpub.com

E-mail: info@bookleafpub.com

ISBN: 9789360945893

First edition 2024

I put a spell on you

I put a spell on you
now it's no ones fault but mine
The chaos and the heartache
all of the unforgiving time
Is the only way out really through?
You put a spell on me and it set you free
though only for a while
Dark emotions swimming among your blood
Help break this curse or we will surely expire

Untitled 1

Shall I compare thee to a summers farm?
Eat me
Breed me
Milk me
Prize?
Pet?
Person?

Know your worth

I do not fear these thorns of mine
they've born from within me
You're still hesitant to shed some blood
so I'd rather watch you leave

Untitled 2

Karma is the universe's way of teaching us that
we reap what we sow
Revenge is the spirits way of teaching us karma
Hell is being caught in the web of both

Witch hunt

Tied to the stake, stuck like herbs to a candle
Oiled, shining, still gleaming in the face of fear
(yours, not mine)
Light a match over my head and watch the wax
drip down...
wax drip down...
wax drip down...
Point my face toward to flame coming my way
"Keep your chin up," they say
"It could always be worse"
Cool breeze
Tight squeeze
Realize far too late what you've done and feel
yourself freeze

Codependency

6

If I'm replaceable,
I'm already dead

Untitled 3

7

If you show up, I'll let you in
Please come home and let's begin again

Your eyes

A vision of green and blue
I've immersed in you
an ocean of a man

Untitled 4

As the teeth rot and fall from my warn down jaw
I blame the things you've done
You blame the past I saw
Like a bee steals from a flower,
my parts have been seduced
You struck my fragile stem to die
with the stinger still left inside
Yet somehow it's you in the end feeling used

Untitled 5

Look up, me! Look up!
What is this that I have stumbled upon?
Clouded skies turned to shades of green
These newfound feelings under a weathered
willow branch
remind me that it's not worth suffering

Rumors

You paint me one way
though I've already been drawn another
Proving what to who?
Why rearrange the prints of blue
when the original is already a work of art

Untitled 6

Under your skin
In your hair
Beneath your nails
Knotted stomach
Wincing eyes
I make you sick, I recognize
Four dry, crusted lips
Rough winds, too strong
Our bodies may never get along

Untitled 7

What else could I have done to save us
aside from nothing at all?
We know that each time that I hit the ground,
it's even farther that you fall
I drag you without purpose
No real answers will you find from me
I'll never know why I act this way
but I know I'm not your destiny
Forgive me
Forgive me
Forgive me
In the end, you should only know the truth
Though what else can I do from here
when you refuse to believe the proof?

Untitled 8

Fuck the beast,
but I'm still a beauty
Claw at your own eyes
You don't deserve to see my face
especially when you make me cry
Who needs your gaze?
Who needs to be worshipped?
Who needs to be assumed for what they're not?
You don't even know me
Back away from the fire
because for you, it's just too hot
Not your muse
Barely art
A car crash in plain sight
I better never hear you say that this was all a
surprise

Soft enough?

You don't have to question yourself anymore
Yes, I am real
And yes, I am alive
Skin, fat, bones and all
I'm not just an idea
This isn't a movie (we could film one if you
want)
Reach through your screen and feel me
Break the barrier with me
Can't you feel me?
Your fingers graze my cheek
Can't you feel me yet?
What does that feel like?
Like everything you ever wanted?
Am I soft enough yet?
I've un furrowed my messy brow for you
Soft enough yet?
I've unclenched my jaw for you
Soft enough yet?
I've wiped the sweat from under my swollen
eyes for you
Soft enough yet?
Slip your fingers through the glass
Promise it won't shatter or crack
Can't guarantee that you won't bleed

Can't you feel me now?
Do you feel like me now when you cross over to
this side?
Does it soften you, too?
Please tell me that it softens you too

What is love?

What is love if not our excuse for every
mistake?
What is love if not the reason for every failed
plan we made?
What is love if our losing hearts never win?
What is love if none of this is justified in the
end?
What is love if not what's lost and rarely what's
been found?
What is love if our curiosity only leads us buried
underground?
What is love if not what guides me through the
darkest nights?
What is love if not the brightest light?
What is love if not what firmly grips my hollow
hands?
What is love if not a calming glance?
What is love if not what holds us down when the
world is determined to make us drown?

Monster

You're repulsed by the weight that I chose to put on
You're repulsed by the mess that I've made and I want
You're repulsed by the love that I need to survive
You're repulsed by the ways that I've learned to get by
You're repulsed by my face, yet you can't look away
Who's really the monster when you treat me like prey?

Gaslit

You left me for dead then wondered how I got
this cold
why my heart stopped working
why the details on my face are drastically
growing old
You left me chained to a tree in the middle of the
night
and never once considered your own sanity
or whether this was morally right
You locked me away inside and swallowed up
the key
making sure no one else would find me
not a soul to hear my pleas
You handed me the knife that cut my skin so
deep
then forced me to hide my scars
yet preach that secrets, we must not keep
You tied me to your bumper and dragged me at
full speed
Still, you tell me I'm taking life too slow
This screams "gaslit" to me

Before you point your finger...

Much to say about when and how I bathe
from the one watching me cleanse without
permission
Who's the asshole?
Much to say about when and where I sleep
from the one watching me rest without
permission
Who's the asshole?
Much to say about my size and shape
from the one with both eyes glued to my scale
without permission
Who's the asshole?
Much to say about the anger I try to suppress
from the soul crusher themself
Who's the asshole?
Much to say about the state of my vagina
(where it's been and with whom)
from those who claim solidarity with, and
freedom for, all women
Who's the asshole?
Much to say from the winners circle
by those who claim they run the winner's circle
run by those who think they run the winners
circle

Asshole or winner?

Now flip your handwritten script for just one day

If I watch you cleanse, am I the winner or the asshole?

If I watch you sleep, am I the winner or the asshole?

If I monitor your scale, am I the winner or the asshole?

If I seclude you and chip away at your lonely soul, am I the winner or the asshole?

If I take a look in your pants and count the rings like an aging tree, am I the winner or the asshole?

Now go collect your award and take a bow, asshole (winner)

Triple Moon Goddess

The moon of three
When you study me, which one do you see?
The maiden, the mother, or the crone?
Don't consider my age
Don't consider my clothes
In my presence, what is it that you seek?
I will share with you nature
I will share with you nurture
I will share with you wisdom beyond belief
But first you must assure me that you trust in the
moon
and the magical powers of three
Three women
Three hearts
Three flowers
Three plots
Three plans to start your life new
So study me and soon you will see
what the moon can also do for you

Awkward/Sexy

Tell me how uncomfortable it makes you when
images of me cross your mind
My awkward, sexy dancing
You wish the brain could go blind
Don't you let the ball drop, honey
Don't you let me stop
Does it make you feel awkward and sexy just as
much as it gets me hot?
Push on through and let's fulfill a twisted fantasy
Maybe it's strange
and oh so wrong
Some tell us it can't be
My moves are slow
My curves are off
Though crooked, you love me
Tell me how weird I make things feel when I'm
awkward and sexy
I must be doing something right if you can't let it
go
I'm haunting you
It's gross, but true
Your awkward, sexy ho

9 789360 945893